Colors of France

A Painting Pilgrimage

Colors of France

A Painting Pilgrimage

MARGARET HALL HOYBACH

AND JOAN BROWN

FIRST LIGHT BOOKS

Seattle, Washington

COVER: *Wall of Camellias*

BACK COVER: *View From the Bridge*, detail of pages 74-75

First Light Books LLC
1426 Harvard Avenue #40
Seattle, Washington 98122-3813

ISBN 0-9717082-0-7

Library of Congress Control Number: 2001099392

Design: Ultragraphics, Los Angeles, California
Photography: Alterman Studios
Printed in China

For orders, call 1-866-FLTBOOK (1-866-358-2665)
or e-mail FirstLightBooks@aol.com

Contents

The Beginning

NOTHING HAPPENS UNLESS FIRST A DREAM.

—Carl Sandburg

The first step of the journey on which I was setting out had really been taken years before—deep inside myself. Never mind that my plane had only now touched down in the French Pyrénées. In my mind, I had begun this pilgrimage a lifetime ago.

I remember going to museums as a child growing up near Washington, D.C., already in love with Monet's work. Like him, I delight in painting flowers. I could spend hours gazing at his Japanese bridge, floating beneath his clouds on the enchanted waters of his water lily pond, savoring the mirror images of reflected wisteria and weeping willow leaves.

The wonder is that reality surpassed the dream, as I sketched my way north along the back roads of France that took me, finally, to Monet's gardens at Giverny.

I don't know that any other trip could be as special as the one that carried me to the land of the Impressionists and to the pink house and gardens of Monet, my favorite among them. It was a dream to which I had not even dared give words because only one seemed to fit—and that was *impossible*.

River walk

The Mythical Kingdom

Sometimes, even seemingly impossible dreams come true. When Patricia, a French-speaking friend in one of my watercolor classes, suggested we go to France together to paint, we set the wheels in motion to do what had once seemed to me forever beyond my reach. From Charleston, South Carolina where I live and work, we have come to St.-Étienne-de-Baïgorry, in the Basque country in the south of France.

Now, we are deep in a France very few get to see. Unlike tour groups and painting expeditions that stray little from the beaten path, we seek out the back roads, setting out for places unknown to either of us. It is early April and we are tracking springtime as it makes its way north.

The gentle world we step into is a realm of red-tiled roofs enfolded in green velvet hills, of Roman bridges and "*Bonjour, Madame*" echoing softly from the lips of total strangers as we stroll about, relishing the feel of the place.

Making our way up a tiny road, the jingle of bells drifts our way, punctuated by the "baahs" of a wall of long-haired woolly sheep that suddenly engulf the road, headed straight for us. Far behind, a *grand-maman* with stick in hand pumps slowly forward on a bicycle, herding the shuffling "dust mops" gently along. Immersed in the stream of warm bodies, we are swept further into this kingdom of farms and sheep and vineyards.

That night we feast on Basque vegetable soup, sole and truffles meunière, beef tournedos and white aspara-gus, each course as much a delight for the eye as the palate. Ravenous for the scene around us as well, we sketch all we can see from the window of the hotel dining room.

By the end of the very first day I've done fourteen
sketches. Still a month away from Giverny, we have
already come to a place that, minute by minute, pelts me
with images crying out, "Paint me! Paint me!" I fall into
bed exhausted, mumbling, "Stop, stop, I can't do it all
at once. I have to sleep now."

View of the town
from the Hôtel Arcé

Sheep and cherry trees

St. Étienne de Baïgorry
from the bridge

Split Second Sketching

There's an excitement in the first sketches I do, an emotional tether to where I am.

When I've just arrived in a place that I've never seen before and set up an easel and all the other things I need to do a full painting on site, it seems to me I'm jumping the gun. It's too soon. I just don't understand the scene yet.

Sketching lends that understanding because I'm recording the impressions coming in upon me. And, unlike a photograph, the passion comes through too.

When I sit down to sketch, there's a spontaneity that comes from each split-second choice I make. I'm going only for the essentials, the magic of the moment, in the first sketch. The white space of information I leave out is almost as important as what I include. And it's all subconscious. This is not the finished painting. There are no worries about perfection. Instead, I record the excitement.

What I sketch says, "This is what I want to paint, this, opposed to everything else around it." What I leave out cuts right to the heart of the world in front of me. The seeds for all my paintings first take root in my painting journal.

Even later, when I do a larger painting from my small color-washed drawings, it is the on-site sketches that carry me back to the intensity of the moment, that breathe life into the later, final depiction of the scene. And once again, I am there.

Roman bridge

Saint-Étienne-de-Baïgorry

Each morning in St.-Étienne we trek through town to buy our loaf of fresh bread for breakfast. Crossing the centuries-old Pont Romain, my mind conjures up the scores of generations who have preceded us across this hump-backed footbridge. Here, where I now walk, the feet of Roman legions have tramped, Gallic lovers sauntered and youngsters frolicked. I can hear the waters of the river beneath me, tumbling by the Hôtel Arcé where we are staying. If I could be unseen, I'd turn cartwheels beside it, so caught up am I in this painting paradise.

Wisteria creeps up the stucco sides of houses. This morning, the figure of a woman is silhouetted against them as she walks home, a long baguette of bread tucked under one arm. At the end of the bridge, a stand of iris trumpets springtime beneath the "turrets" of roofs and green hills. And everywhere lilacs and camellias caress hot whitewashed walls splashed with deep lavender shadows. Small wonder Monet tried to "catch hold" of light—such light—and fling it onto canvas.

Here, easels are as common as trees. As I set up to work on the bridge and along the river, passers-by smile and nod, chanting their "*Bonjour, bonjour.*" Soon, a small crowd gathers, eager to see what I am doing. For establishing rapport, the next best thing to Pat's French is my sketchbook.

Like a proud Gallic face, the profile of St.-Étienne seems defined by its church spires and arched bridge. Nearby, a 17th-century château stands abandoned by all but the spirits still mourning the passing of the last son of the ruling

Window at the
Hotel Arcé.

Patriz, the burly Basque artist who works and lives here with his mother, does watercolors and masterful sculpture. Hidden away in a tiny studio in the hills and very successful, he is all that one fantasizes a French artist to be. I cannot resist acquiring a landscape he has done in watercolor, pen and ink—about the size of a sketchbook page. The technique so catches my eye that I'm inspired to begin enlarging my own black and white sketches from thumbnail size, adding watercolor to them right on scene as often as possible. Patriz speaks no English; his mother, only a smattering. But artists tell their stories best without words. Perhaps that is why our encounter leaves me so willing to change my long-established technique of recording the moment.

Farther down the lane we discover a cemetery—its tombstones inscribed in Basque. We are just minutes from the Spanish border. Our explorations have led us to a hilltop overlooking all of St.-Étienne. What joy to be perched on this aerie from which to sketch the scene below. Sun-dappled trees frame the waters rushing

family. His fall from a parapet left it ownerless, empty and for sale. The perfect setting for a Gothic romance.

Exploring the country lanes about fifteen miles outside of town, we spot a tiny sign that reads *Atelier*, signaling we have stumbled upon an artist's studio. We scurry along an ever-narrowing dirt path as it leads up the hill to a large house and a small outbuilding, veiled by an orchard of flowering fruit trees.

Cascading lilacs

Fireplace

beneath the bridge built by the Romans, as if directing attention to the Basque church's steeple.

Everywhere you look, the Pyrénées around us glow with springtime bloom—clematis, azalea, peonies, tulips and pansies. Fishermen stand waist-deep in mountain streams, angling for trout. Our timing could not have been better.

Each evening we probe deeper into the mountains, past the trout farms, pampering our palates with

Basque scallops, salad niçoise or some of the splendid fresh catches.

Caught up as we are, we leave the magic of this place with great reluctance. We would gladly stay longer if we did not have the gardens at Giverny, and so much en route, to lure us onward.

Five days earlier, when we first arrived, all anyone at the Hôtel Arcé had asked of us was, "Mesdames, would you like a room?" They'd imprinted no credit card, held no passport, required no identification.

It hadn't mattered that I could speak so little French. A palette was all it took to open hearts and doors. And we found it all totally amazing.

yellow fields

cherry trees

Basque countryside

Mountain stream en route
to La Mongie

La Mongie

To our surprise, after journeying northward, we are greeted with still more warmth than that which has buoyed our first days in country. Just outside of Tarbes, French friends offer us the use of the family's ski chalet in the mountains in which to paint.

Giddy with the possibilities, we can hardly wait to set up easels atop La Mongie. Still snow-covered, these Pyrénées peaks tower above now-green valleys burgeoning with mauves, golds and magentas. A gray stone church nestles against the base of the mountain. And again, there are sheep to add their woolly welcome.

Halfway to the top, we find ourselves shaded by trees blushing with apple blossoms. Basking in the warmth, we pause beside a canopied brook that invites painting and picnicking on petite quiche picked up at the *pâtisserie*. We lunch, perched mid-stream on a rock, to the sounds of solitude, punctuated by the flutelike serenading of birds in the trees beneath which we rest. Our joy in the gift of this rare opportunity seems echoed in the beauty surrounding us.

We can't resist whooping it up with a shirtsleeved snowball fight, scooping up the winter residue at the side of the road for ammunition. A canvas of azure sky stretches above, yielding no hint to cease our dallying.

We arrive at nightfall, eager to tumble into bed for an early awakening. We will not forfeit a moment of the chance to capture the panoramic scene stretched out around and below us.

Instead, we awaken to discover it is we who have been captured. Rubbing our early-morning eyes does nothing to dislodge the white mantle we see shrouding us. In the night, a spring blizzard has whited out our vistas.

For the next three days, we find ourselves snowed in on the mountain. Meal by meal, the pasta we dig out of a chalet cabinet grows more dreary. A shopping expedition planned for the day after our arrival is now impossible. We have neither boots with which to mush through the three-foot-drifts to a nearby store nor chains to carry our rental car safely back down the mountain. Worst of all, both mountain peaks and floral splendor are lost in the snow. The world before us is itself a blank canvas.

When a St. Bernard trots out of the hoary mists past our door, we hope, in vain, for the mythical brandy or food. Our hosts phone anxiously from Tarbes "You've *got* to come down from the mountain to stay with us."

The concierge of the ski apartments, once apprised of our plight, agrees to undertake our rescue, shoveling us out of the deep snow, then driving us in his car to rendezvous with our friends at the foot of the mountain. Our buried rental car can be picked up later.

White-knuckled, we hang on for dear life to the sides of the four-wheel-drive in which we are swirling down the slopes, around and around icy hairpin spirals. If this is a near-death experience, I hope beyond hope to be embraced by the promised light at the end of a seemingly endless whirling passage.

Incredibly, when we emerge, intact, it is to just such a loving embrace, in a world bright with warmth, color—and food. Even the peacocks strolling Tarbes' city parks, abloom with tulips, magnolia and cherry trees, seem dreamlike. For the next few days our hosts share with us a generous slice of French suburban life.

It seems fitting that it is Easter on which we celebrate with them in the serenity of Gregorian chant as the voices of nuns float from behind cloistered Carmelite walls at a convent near Lourdes. Miracles

Gray stone church

and salvation never seemed more at hand.

Later in the day, the town heralds the vernal rebirth of life with a parade. A teddy bear rides the front of a tractor as teenagers glide by on bicycles or farm machinery resplendent with flowers, branches of trees and crepe paper. 3-D *joie de vivre*!

Now, feasting replaces famine as we gather at the family table for home cooking fit for a gourmand. We are only at the aperitifs and what I see convinces me this is where our St. Bernard made all his deliveries.

I count eight brandy bottles lined up and we are to sample every one. With each tasting, my French sounds better to me. For those I'm meeting for the first time, my memorized lines roll off my lips, "I am an artist traveling through France to paint in Monet's gardens" and "I have a husband who is a pilot and three children at university in the United States." Mysteriously, it comes out as, "I have three husbands and a child attending a supermarket in the United States."

Undaunted, our hosts persist in including me in the meal-time chatter. In addition to French, the daughter speaks English and Spanish; the mother, Spanish; the father, German.

Years ago I studied Spanish and German, to which I've recently added fractured French phrases. Now, rather than embarrass me by translating my English to French, each dinner companion converses with me in whatever language is common to us, making me feel a part of things. Combinations of French, Spanish and German reel around the table, changing as often as speakers, as each course progresses.

Now *Monsieur Le Poisson* is laid out before us with head and tail intact. What we are about to enjoy is itself a work of art, but making eye contact with my food is a new experience. The exquisite pastries with which we complete the meal are far more impersonal but no less spectacular.

Our Tarbes friends indulge me with such a potpourri of tongues and gracious inclusion, I dub them the "United Nations family." As far as I am concerned, they are fluent, above all else, in the universally understood language of kindness.

Wildflowers of the Pyrénées

Guittard Farm

Cliffhangers

The mountains flatten into rolling hills as we head north into the farmlands of central France, only to discover just about everything is closed because of the Easter holidays. The gas gauge warns us we're in peril of ending up stranded by the side of the road, while our stomachs shrink back to La Mongie starving artist size. As if that were not enough—we are lost.

With our only clue a guidebook listing of a bed and breakfast called *Chez Guittard*, we finally ferret out the family farm and hamlet of four *petites maisons* clustered high in the hills of Castang. Once again we have the good fortune to alight high atop a bluff, overlooking vintage stone farm buildings and a countryside that, for most visitors, remains hidden. Here one can surely put a finger on the pulse of rural France.

But on this day, putting our hands on some food is something else again. In a central eating area stand both a fireplace and a stove on which we are free to cook. Once settled in, we drive back to a nearby town to begin a three-hour search for an open market in which to buy something to prepare. Not wanting to waste another minute of gorgeous weather on what is clearly "mission impossible," we abandon the effort, going back to bread, water, seven-day-old prunes from the mountaintop—and painting.

Just a few feet from our bedroom window, Patric Guittard is pushing his formidable cow into a stall in the barn mucked out earlier in the day by Madame. Again I find that even the buildings of this gentler world fascinate

"Lace curtains"
View from my bedroom

me and decide to begin painting from the inside, looking out. The late afternoon shifting of light and shadow leaves me as breathless as the panorama before me. No wonder art is a national pastime for the French.

Our room is on the path to the common bathroom and squeaky boards herald the approach of one and all users. We spend the night squirming for comfort in a shared three-quarter bed, awakening to the creaks of the hall floor, until totally roused from early morning slumber by the mooing and crowing below us. "You know," I say sleepily to Pat, "maybe we should upgrade our room half a star—just so we can have two beds." We arise sleep-deprived and famished—but laughing.

The usual French breakfast includes coffee, bread, jam and butter, with an

Monique and "Pamplouf"

Rocamadour stairs

occasional cheese. To this, Madame Guittard adds hot porridge, served by the fireside. Glorious painting weather proves the ultimate restorative, especially when, knowing my love of flowers, Madame Guittard carries in a bunch of amethyst iris she has picked for me to paint.

A grand cat sitting in the window of one of the other little neighboring houses catches my eye later in the morning as I'm out for a walk. I pause to admire the charm of the framed scene, only to discover Monique, its owner, has appeared as well and is beckoning me to enter. A fireplace, copper pots and vases of flowers fill the tiny kitchen of the charming two-room stone-walled house. In the bedroom , I discover a four-poster bed covered with tapestries and quilts, the centerpiece of which is a basket of six newborn kittens, offspring of the proud mother cat basking in the sunlight of the window. As we sit chatting around the basketed babies on Madame's bed, I am ecstatic to learn I can speak to this kind woman in my native tongue, for she is a teacher of English. Once again, out of the blue, a strand of hospitality is tied like a ribbon around a piece of our journey.

At lunchtime, we begin our exploration of nearby Sarlat and the prehistoric caves etched by artists of another millennium. A neighboring medieval city is built into the sides of bluffs. In Rocamadour, we thread our way through the limestone hills above the Alzou valley, along a single narrow street—just two or three people wide—to paint at the top. The rapid pulse, caught breath and sense of exhilaration that I feel are from joy rather than altitude. Here, castle ramparts overlook the basilica that stands watch over this cliff-clinging ancient village. The terrain sucks up rainwater like a sponge. Below, a parched river creeps along the canyon floor.

From here, we are expected in Limoges. Who would want to miss visiting a porcelain factory and exploring studio shops? I am acquiring a collection of French blues—first a tablecloth, then some Quimper pottery. To my already overloaded knapsack, I now add a jewel of an enamel. Its white wild flowers, etched into turquoise and royal blue, catch my eye because they are the subject of my own *Queen Anne's Court* watercolor.

We are ever mindful of our mission though and, no matter what the enticement, must not linger. We embark on a back road route still farther north, pausing often to paint. It turns into what seems a never ending day on the road and we long for the *pâté de foie*

Rocamadour

gras and other delicacies that have pampered our palates at Au Moulin de la Gorce outside Limoges. Again thwarted in our efforts to find markets open when we need food, we graze on whatever is at hand, picnicking on dregs of fish pie and brioche, garnished by the last of the expired La Mongie prunes. Fasting, it seems, is also a necessary part of pilgrimage.

Afternoon thunderstorm
Île d'Yeu

Painting as a Second Language

A dinner of *galatea crêpes* and ratatouille restores us at the *crêperie* of the hotel at which we are spending the night. Despite the fact that every truck in France grinds by under our window, we are fascinated by this area of small coastal towns. In the early morning, we plan to embark to Île d'Yeu, a tiny Atlantic island.

On the way to the ferry, Pat drops off to stand in line for tickets while I pop into a pharmacy to refill an antibiotic prescription a French doctor has prescribed for an infection I've developed. Pat assures me all I have to do is go in, hand the pharmacist the prescription and they'll give me the medicine, without my having to say a word.

Instead, I get a torrent of French as to why they can't fill it. As my frustration and desperation grow, I stammer a scramble of Spanish, French and English, *"Un momento, yo tengo une amie who habla français muy bien,"* at which everybody in the store bursts into laughter. Thankfully, one of the customers has a smattering of English, takes pity on me and offers to help translate so that I can get my medicine, just in time to make a mad dash for the dock.

Île d'Yeu's red-tiled rooftops and vine-covered, white-washed walls give it a tropical look, much like a Greek isle somehow displaced from the Aegean Sea. As other visitors bicycle the island's short length—no cars allowed here, I stroll, knapsack on my back, to paint the beaches, a harbor filled with flag-flying boats and outdoor cafes overflowing, from morning to night, with people and mouth-watering delectables. Waves of color dance in the waters as I sit painting in the harbor. A cup of tea warms me up from a cool morning of sketching.

Harbor at Île d'Yeu

Shadows

Climbing roses and white washed walls

"Bon appétit!"

le père

le grand-père

la fille

La famille

"Dick"
le chien

40

Beach at Île d'Yeu

On an island as we are, the seafood is so fresh we gorge ourselves on mussels. It isn't until I've finished painting for the day that I allow myself to sit, people-watching, over un *verre de vin blanc*.

Returning to the mainland that evening, I escape the gnawing seasickness that filled my hour and a half boat trip over earlier in the day. The challenge of using my halting French distracts me from what the seas are doing, while my sketchbook helps me make quick friends of a local family on holiday, even though they speak no English.

At first I begin to draw them almost surreptitiously. In many places in the world, people don't like to be sketched. But I decide to ask permission. Their smiling approval allows me to pencil in portraits of *grand-maman* and papa, mother and a bearded father, a young daughter and Dick, the dog. The French, I find, take their dogs everywhere.

Continuing north along the scenic route, I stop to paint windmills on the way to Nantes, where we are staying overnight with another family of friends. They include us in a gathering of three generations at a Sunday dinner of salmon, white asparagus and fresh-picked strawberries. Even in the short time of our visit, I find myself swept away by the contrast between the warmth of the welcome we receive and the Gallic detachment I had anticipated. How far I have come too, adding so much to the nature subjects that had come to pre-empt my palette in recent years. I find myself embarked on a journey of interior as well as exterior discovery.

We are on our way to Monet's world-famous gardens yet, all along the way, consummate plantings bloom everywhere. I find it almost hard to believe the black tulips and orange azaleas of Nantes' Le Jardin Des Plantes are real. As guest at an artistic banquet that has only just begun, I find even the "hors d'oeuvres" a *tour de force* and I am breathless in anticipation of all that is still to come.

"Le moulin de vent
The windmill

Blue shutters
on windmill

Chapel at Château Brélidy

Arthurian Trails

I've painted before in England. Now I'm on the other side of the Channel, sketching along the rocky shores of the westernmost part of France, an area steeped in the legend of Arthur. He is said to have criss-crossed this section of Brittany in travels with his knights of the round table. Perhaps, in my own way, I too am journeying in search of a "holy grail." Here slate-roofed stone buildings replace the red tile and whitewash of those in the warmer south. There is an aura of strength and mystery to both people and place.

The day we arrive, after a long drive through the Brittany countryside, our eyes are suddenly drawn to a long arcade of cherry trees, just beginning to burst forth with blossoms. Almost as if parting the mists of the past, their cotton candied branches point skyward to where we are headed, a hillside château overlooking tiny Brélidy.

At least as far back as university days, European history has captured my imagination. Now I stand atop the ruins of a 14th-century mound, looking back across the moat area to the 16th-century château in which we are staying. I can see the foundations where turrets have extended and, in my mind's eye, men, perhaps armed with picks, running up the hill.

For all the peacefulness of the cherry blossom-draped countryside, one can sense an intrusion: on the side of the hill, bunkers from recent world wars are still plainly visible. Conflicts have shattered this serenity, time after time, for hundreds of years. How do these people, who look so at peace, put their lives back together again—and again and again?

It could be that they find solace in the small chapel secreted in these now quiet woods, its statues and stained glass windows still in place. Tending history in one's own backyard surely lends perspective. Or perhaps their secret lies in treasuring the present moment.

Since beginning my journey, I, too, see in a different light. My pen and brush record the excitement in the sketches that fill the pages of my books. For the first time in twenty years, the shapes of things creep into my garden of flowers and find a place of welcome: the fireplace in St.-Étienne, the windows of the hotel, the dining room scene, a bowl and pitcher here in Brélidy. A suit of armor clamors to be painted next.

Pol-de-Léon, the château's resident ghost of a sixteen-year-old soldier, who came from a neighboring area to fight, proves too elusive for me. Carefully opening the door to the chamber off the billiard room, where our gracious innkeeper, Eliane Yoncourt, has felt his presence, I can tune in to no one.

On the landing just outside our room, antique beds are bedecked with age-old lace wedding dresses, christening gowns and other relics of past occupants. Unlike our elusive ghost, these vestiges of turning points in the lives of others do reach out to touch me. Once these garments held the hearts and yearnings of women and children who climbed these same stone steps that now lead to my fourth floor room. They too stood before its casement windows, looking out on the village beyond. How did it look then?

Windows, and the scenes framed by them, appear more and more often in the pages of my sketchbook. One afternoon I decide to work from inside the château, pushing open the shutters on the nearby landing to sketch the view of the town, a blue and white pitcher in the foreground. As I do, one of the pigeons that nests just beneath the roof eaves darts into the room.

My paints are spread out all over the stone floor at the top of a stairway leading up to the small area in which I am sitting to paint. But I am no longer alone. My winged companion circles madly about me,

View of Brélidy· from the Château

swooping over the carefully laid out dresses, batting up against the walls, round and round, as I hear Madame just below us. She is on her way up, conducting guests on a tour of the château.

"Go away, go away," I shout, trying to recall the French "*Vas-y, vas-y*," which I have heard used on another occasion. But all in vain, for my French bird refuses to respond until the group is only a few steps below, gaping at the strange American, hopping madly about among her paints, noisily trying to evict a just-departed, seemingly non-existent, creature. There is no one else here to explain, my own pigeon French being totally inadequate to the task.

Mortified, I sit back down on the floor to paint again as the entourage descends, with much discreet head-shaking. I can understand just enough to make out Madame extolling the talents of this visiting, if eccentric, artiste. Right down to her fingertips, our hostess exudes charm, much like the château itself.

We'd called ahead, the afternoon of the day we drove to Brélidy, when we realized we were going to be arriving later than planned. Assuring us we need not worry, Madame said she would prepare "just a little light supper" when we got there, so we would be sure not to starve.

She welcomed us to the stone-walled château in which we were to be so comfortably ensconced, serving us an aperitif to warm us, as we settled in before the blazing fireplace. Soup, salad, cheese and dessert followed. So much for "light."

Each morning of our five-day sojourn begins with a breakfast of croissants, *beurre* and *confiture*. I have forgotten that cholesterol even exists. It is then, too, that we get to choose the seafood or meat to go with the many delightful accompaniments that will greet us at a bountiful evening meal. Throughout each day's scouting out of the area's treasures, we look forward to coming home to what we have chosen, knowing that Madame herself will carry the meals to us in the elegance of the château dining room.

On a side trip to the coast, near Perros-Guirec, we scramble among menhirs, coppery-pink mammoth rocks

Anna's gate

bizarrely scattered on the beach, as if set down hurriedly by giants interrupted in their task of constructing a second Stonehenge, this time on French shores. Not far from here is the megalith said to be the tomb of Arthur. Everywhere we explore along this chilly coast we stumble upon another place reputed to be the scene of the king's mythic quest and adventures.

Another outing, this time without a sea sick ferry ride, takes us among scattered reefs and small islands to Île de Bréhat. No cars are allowed here either and we walk and sketch the day away among just blooming hydrangea, cormorants and lofty cliffs. Lots of little walkways with high walls give evidence of the French love of enclosed gardens. The appetite we soon work up is more than satisfied by a massive pizza, topped with shrimp, calamari and an assortment of other seafood brought in from local waters.

The days we spend closer to the château, a two-mile walk takes us to town. Preparing to sketch a little fence scene of flowers and stone wall by the side of a road where it's clear livestock pass through, I sit carefully, mindful of nearby piles of cow manure. Further into town the next day, we stop outside a garden, and walk to its wrought-iron gate, drawn by a huge blanket of clematis hanging over the walls. "This is where I want to paint," I whisper, feeling very much at home with this little pocket of Charleston-like beauty. Yet, you never know how someone on the other side of a wall, behind which a dog is barking, might react to my setting up right there.

Suddenly, the gate swings open. With the help of a cane, Anna, a tiny, silver-haired woman in peddle pushers, makes her way out from behind her walled yard, smiling broadly and talking to me a mile a minute in French. She gestures not to include her in my painting because she is too undone from working in the garden. More insistently, she invites me into her home for a coffee break.

With Pat off painting some distance away, I sputter my few phrases, "I am an artist, painting in France," and "we are going to *les jardins de Monet*." Even with no one on hand to interpret, Anna continues to go out of her way to welcome me, an American stranger who has appeared at her gate and speaks almost no French. I wonder would we do the same.

I have come to France forewarned to expect coldness or, at best, disinterest. I've not even dared hope for such open arms, such grace. (I believe the French can read the weather report and make it sound like a sonnet.) Whether friend or stranger, each person we have met wants to see us enjoy our visit. Perhaps one could expect it of an innkeeper or long-time friend. Yet, even when things outside of anyone's control aren't going right, the attitude is, "Let us help make it better for you; come, enjoy our country." Anna's gestures of invitation speak volumes: "Please, please come in and join me for some refreshments."

We end up not only staying for lunch but invited back to Anna's stately home the next day to meet monsieur and, on still another occasion, all the grandchildren. The spacious French kitchen, hung with gleaming copper pans and baskets, seems to open its ample arms to clasp us as well. Together, we eat, drink aperitif and raise our glasses to each *"Vive la France,"* *"salut"*ing not only our host country but everywhere else that a long row of brandy bottles can inspire monsieur to toast. Inside her enchanting garden world, Anna makes us the gift of a France we'd never hoped to share.

Lace and peonies

A New Perspective

I've never wanted to paint flowers in vases. Clematis climbing fences, long-stemmed iris against a garden wall, wildflowers clumped by the side of the road, birds in the marshes, seashells by the seashore—nature seduces my eye and my brush.

But rain and a week amidst the antiquities of France changed all that forever. Like a well-aged wine that whets the appetite, these interiors now draw me inside. In the dining room of this fairy-tale château, we inquire, "Madame, would you mind if we paint in here this morning? We will protect the lace tablecloth with plastic."

The room is aglow with the pink and burgundy of a bouquet of peonies, the rosy hues of a nearby brocade chair, and a tablecloth whose blush tones peak through the sheer lace overlay, sculpted in peony blossoms, that tops it. There are gold candelabra, a crystal vase holding the flowers and, along with the glowing fireplace, all is reflected in a gold-edged mirror—definitely not an easy scene to paint.

Yet I want to do it so much I can hardly stand it. Between breakfast and dinner—no lunch is served—I am going to paint this scene, or die in the attempt.

red roof
tan Bldg.

yellow
field

En route to Giverny

Pink fields of flowers

Giverny: The End of the Rainbow

THE SOUL WOULD HAVE NO RAINBOW HAD THE EYES NO TEARS.

—Author Unknown

Coming to Giverny to paint inside Monet's magnificently restored gardens is a pilgrimage, a journey to the Impressionists' mecca, the chance to touch a relic of the man the Western world has canonized as its most beloved painter.

Before going, an artist must first submit work to be juried. We began a year ahead. Once the coveted permission was granted, and throughout the first four weeks of our trip, I murmur an increasingly earnest litany, "Please let me stay well. Let nothing happen to keep me away. Just let me get to Giverny. Even if I have to crawl in on my hands and knees."

By the time we leave Brélidy for our two-week finale in Monet's gardens, the excitement in me builds to such a pitch that we stop only to buy a picnic dinner of barbecued chicken and an unwrapped loaf of French bread at one of the little *pâtisseries* along the way. Beside a Norman church that dates back to 1000 A.D., we eat and sketch in a field carpeted with flowers. It helps to restore equilibrium.

We are billeted in rooms about five miles out from the gardens, on Andersen Farm. A cluster of 17th-century stone buildings, it is run by Patricia and Ian, an English couple who retired here to raise horses. We have two bedrooms with a kitchen in between, a little apartment which we take care of and in which we can do our own cooking. Of the five or six units in this walled complex, ours is over the stables. It seems appropriate. Monet painted in a barn.

For four weeks our meals have ricocheted between gourmet cuisine and those we cobble together ourselves. Here, it is strictly "garbage soup," as we daily extend the stew from a simmered chicken with whatever vegetables and condiments are at hand to make a quick and inexpensive evening meal.

The sounds that awaken me the first night convince me my roommate is in the bathroom, sick. Concerned, I call out, "Pat. . . . Pat. . . . Are you all right?"

A huge whinny, the only reply, follows clamping horse's feet, much like the sound effects of an old Western radio show. It is my four-legged neighbor beneath me that is having trouble sleeping. He is no longer the only one awake.

"God, you look awful," a healthy Pat greets me the next morning.

"My horse kicked all night," I groan. Below us are three Polish steeds, like us, newly arrived.

At the end of each day, I fall into bed, aching to rest, only to be roused by my horse stomping his hooves, banging a feed bucket as he punches his nose into it for oats, answering the calls of nature. Some days Pat's downstairs "neighbor" is up all night too.

It isn't as if there is anything we can do about it, but it does take some getting used to. Unlike a snoring husband, I can't poke this noisemaker to turn over so I can go back to sleep. Patricia and Ian are also having problems with "our" horses, trying to train them. They are proving to be very frisky in the daylight hours too, bolting about as if ready to head for freedom—and Poland.

A beehive, a gigantic sheep dog named Sultan, and Hillary, a fifteen-year-old hen whose company we enjoy as she watches us paint, make up the rest of our menagerie. Best of all are the English cutting gardens, a kaleidoscope of color on the side of a hill. During the hours we can't work in Monet's gardens, because they are open to the public, we come back home to paint.

Although we are only five miles from Giverny, our drive each way takes some twenty minutes on winding

My room

Andersen Farm

"Sultan and Hillary"

country lanes. But what a lovely unexpected gift, each morning of these first two weeks of May. As we come over the hill to Cherence, the town's church steeple and roofs rise out of the yellow fields, emerging from the mists—a kind of Brigadoon. On our way one Sunday morning, we stop here to paint by the side of the road. A mini-Tour de France—at least fifty bicyclers—whips by as church bells peal.

Painting in Giverny is the pièce de résistance of our daily delights. But the other gardens here at the start of the Impressionists' trail at Vétheuil, also settings for famous paintings, tempt our palettes as well. I spend every possible second in Monet's gardens, the rest amidst neighboring floral splendor—painting, painting, painting.

Each morning we leave Andersen Farm about seven, arriving at Giverny in time to walk in with the first gardener to open the service gate. Artists may work from eight in the morning until ten, when we must give way to the throngs eager to tour Monet's place of inspiration.

After two hours of painting, we pack up all of our equipment and leave to sketch our way home.

We drive just across the river, to Vernon, one of Monet's other painting sites, where it's outdoor market day. Here, one can again feel the heartbeat of the local scene. I begin sketching people as they bustle amongst fresh whole fish or chickens hanging high from stalls cheek-to-cheek with other booths from which bustiers and other undergarments sway in the breeze. From cabbages to jeans, my pen can barely keep up with the flurry of activity. Such a contrast with my pre-pilgrimage peaceful landscape scenes. What I am sketching blazes the trail for a whole new series of market scene paintings.

As if obsessed, my pen or brush is at work every conscious moment of the day. At a little before six in the evening, we are back, impatient for the last tourists to leave Giverny so we can begin to paint in the evening light. We stay until we can no longer see to work, about nine or nine-thirty.

Cherence, Sunday morning....
churchbells ringing!

Market day at Vernon

Door at Vétheuil

Yet, in the first moments of that first day, I produce only tears. Alone, seated on Monet's green bridge, I look out over his pond at the water lilies he painted, scenes I have grown up committing to memory, wishing I were there. Now that I am, how have I become so presumptuous as to think I could come here to paint?

Though Monet's words echo through my mind like a mantra, "Try to forget what it is you've got in front of you . . .", I find myself unable. "Just think: here is a little square of blue, an oblong of pink, a streak of yellow, and paint exactly what you see." My host's words, remembered, turn back the intervening years, weaving an aura of century-old welcome over the scene, reminding me of what else I have forgotten. Monet has always invited others here to paint. Now, I too am to be included. At peace, I can finally begin.

I set up first in the water garden because, of all the sites, it is my favorite. Monet's collection of Japanese wood block engravings, still hanging in his pink house, is witness to his love of Asian art. I too bask in its

simplicity, embodied here, and in the endless ballet of light and shadow before me.

At any hour, a soft glow bathes the gardens, a light so unique it lends mystique to the contours of the lush plantings. I paint what I see from a distance, then move closer. Even a few meters lends a new perspective, funneling radiance through a different filter. Wisteria, lilac and iris are each in full bloom, a cloak of cascading lavenders, draping and framing the green overpass.

The view from the bridge itself threatens to undo me once again. Here I sit, hardly another soul around, on the very bridge from which Monet himself has painted, immersed in the setting he created, the subject of so many of his paintings. Why then can I not see it as my host did? Again his words gently prod, ". . . and paint exactly what you see." Surely, granting a guest permission to be herself is the greatest hospitality one can encounter.

It is only on Mondays, when the gardens are closed to everyone else, that we can stay the day. We do not

Gate at Vétheuil

11

even break for meals. An apple, sandwich or candy bar sustains us. Food is secondary to the need to savor this Eden.

On the first of our Mondays, despite the rules, a special busload of tourists is allowed in. With some twenty minutes to see the gardens and find "the perfect spot" for a snapshot, they are oblivious to the fact they are standing on an artist's paintings.

"Excuse me, excuse me, just a minute," I hasten to move out of their way. But no one understands or cares. The invasion ends as rapidly as it begins. Undaunted, I paint out the heel marks.

A French artist, Pierre Bittar, who travels from Versailles most Mondays to paint here in oils on colossal canvases, stops to look at my work and critique it. To my surprise, what I take away from our time together is the decision to begin painting in oils once again, after twenty-five years of painting only watercolors.

I awaken on the last Monday, chilled at the thought of our impending departure, as well as by cold weather outside. I dress in layers: long johns, jeans, a shirt, two sweaters, coat, hat and gloves. With so much to put on, I decide to forego a bra.

At the gardens, I soon learn we are not totally alone this week either. Television cameras are staked out, recording the artists at work, for educational television. Having just emerged, perspiring, from my woolly cap as the day heats up, I am less than enthusiastic at the prospect of being filmed. I wait until the crew leaves the spot in which I want to paint before I move in to set up.

As I work, and the day gets hotter and hotter, I begin to strip. First the coat, one sweater, then the next. Still burning, I toss off the shirt, leaving on just a skimpy undershirt. Unencumbered, and much cooler, I get back to painting, grateful to be alone. Dressed as I am, I'd fit better into an underwear commercial than I do on educational television. Given the dress—or undress—on some European beaches, I wonder why I'm even giving it a second thought.

Green door

Perhaps because I sense I am no longer alone. The crew has spotted me and is hastening back to film me working. To my horror, I realize I can control neither their approach nor what is going on with my scantily clad bosom. Cameras roll for a full half-hour, and I'm exhausted from the effort of trying to paint with my arms across my chest.

In most ways, I do better at conforming to local convention. Many of the gardeners, I learn, descend from a long line of Giverny caretakers. Coming back after hours to fish, they offer their own appraisals of my day's painting. As dusk creeps in, only the drone of present-day traffic outside the walls intrudes on the quiet. A car stops and a door slams. The curious driver scrambles up the enclosure to peer inside. Embarrassed by my being there to see him, he quickly drops down and drives off.

A large trout leaps out of the pond, splashing me back into the moment. Next, a muskrat paddles by, his tiny head parting the retreating water lilies. The next morning, even in the rain and cold, I cannot stop.

Beneath an umbrella, I juggle a brush, palette, paper and easel, watercolors streaming down along with raindrops. In the diffused light of the murky morning, the air heavy with the fragrance and memories of flowers that grew so beautifully in my own grandmother's garden, *Lavenders of Giverny* takes form.

At first, I hate the willows. I cannot "get hold" of them. Why did Monet plant such a tree? They will not let me leave them alone. I keep trying. With each attempt I get more of the feel of it, capturing the luxurious droop of the branches, the profound serenity of all that surrounds me. A gardener steers his green, square-ended rowboat, a replica of Monet's, gliding into the middle of the pond to clear underwater weeds from the water lilies. Each passing cloud and fluttering breeze reflects in the mirror-waters.

By morning light, I sketch in the Clos Normand. Funette and Fifi, the resident mousers, keep me company as I begin to paint the tulips, our host's pink house in the background. There is almost too much

Monet's house at Giverny

Approach to the bridge

View from the bridge

Weeping willows

to choose from in gardens that are themselves
a masterpiece.

"I am no good at anything but painting and
gardening," Monet once said of himself. The world has
found it more than enough—and beaten a path to this
doorstep I am sketching.

Here, reality outstrips expectation, unlike a coveted
prize that, once won, disappoints. Yet, I have only begun
to scratch the surface. Even before I leave this painter's
paradise, I hunger to return. As I walk out the gate
for this last time, I can hear the whispers, urging me
back, "Paint me, paint me."

Arbor in front garden

My heart is always, always at giverny.

—Claude Monet